God's Paintbrush

TEACHER'S GUIDE

A Guide for Jewish and Christian Educators and Parents

Edited by Rabbi Jeffrey L. Schein & Rabbi Joseph M. Blair

Contributors:

Renée Frank Holtz
Elizabeth McMahon Jeep
Rabbi Sandy Eisenberg Sasso
Rabbi Jeffrey L. Schein
Alice Weinstein

God's Paintbrush Teacher's Guide:
A Guide for Jewish and Christian Educators and Parents

2001 Third Printing
1997 Second Printing
1996 First Printing

First Edition

Manufactured in the United States of America
Design by Maria O'Donnell

For People of All Faiths, All Backgrounds
Published by Jewish Lights Publishing
www.jewishlights.com

Contents

Preface

Rabbi Jeffrey L. Schein

This teacher's guide is a result of several versions of a course entitled "Theological Quests and Developmental Questions" taught by Dr. Jeffrey Schein and Roberta Louis Goodman. Two of these courses were sponsored by the Reconstructionist Rabbinical College and the Federation of Reconstructionist Congregations and Havurot (FRCH). The third was sponsored by the Cleveland College of Jewish Studies and the Cleveland Fellows Program.

Within each of these courses, a significant amount of time was devoted to exploring *God's Paintbrush* as a way of presenting God to children. Participants watched teachers read and explore *God's Paintbrush* with children between the ages of 7 and 10. Alice Weinstein's list of ways to "extend the learning" came out of her observations of this teaching. The suggestions in the sections on "Varying the Learning" by Jeffrey Schein reflect the discussion and analysis of several dozen teachers who also commented on what they observed about the response of children to the book. "The Family Program" was initiated by Renée Frank Holtz under the guidance of Dr. Sherri Blumberg, Professor of Education at Hebrew Union College–Jewish Institute of Religion.

Because *God's Paintbrush* is a book for people of all faiths we have included in this guide the section by Elizabeth McMahon Jeep, "Teaching Suggestions for Christian Educators." We think it would be interesting and appropriate if Jewish and Christian educators and parents would read through all of the sections of the guide, as there may very well be ideas that each can borrow from the other and adapt to their own tradition.

Children will color their discussions about God from the palette of their particular religious symbols and traditions. Even as they speak out of their own religious experience they will come to realize that there is one God to whom we all belong.

Introduction: The Author's Intent

Rabbi Sandy Eisenberg Sasso

No child reaches school age without having constructed an image or images of God. Regardless of religious instruction, children think about God. Teachers and other adults need to decide how they can best help young people in their religious search. Regrettably, our own feelings of inadequacy in theological discussions restrain us from conversations about God with our children. Our children, in turn, learn that God is something about which no one wants to talk. Their God ideas are formed without benefit of adult guidance and often result in superstitious beliefs and immature theologies. These beliefs are frequently abandoned because they cannot grow or sustain our youngsters through the journey to adulthood.

God's Paintbrush is meant to encourage a conversation about God with children. Since children arrange abstract ideas in concrete ways, *God's Paintbrush* provides a variety of pictures, divine images which arise out of ordinary childhood experiences. These pictures or metaphors are meant to encourage children's religious imaginations, to help them see God in the loving acts of parents, in nature and in themselves. By offering a variety of metaphors, the book moves beyond the singular graying grandfather image and suggests that there are many ways of naming God. A multiplicity of metaphors is a reminder that each image is incomplete, a partial pointing to God.

Religious tradition is steeped in God metaphors. The generation of the Red Sea called God, Redeemer. The generation of Sinai called God, Teacher. At the rivers of Babylon, the people called God, Comforter. Those who lived off the land called God, Shepherd. What we call something, how we name it, is to a great extent what it is to us. *God's Paintbrush* helps children say what and who God is to them. It gives youngsters a language with which to speak about God.

When asked to picture who God is, many children will draw an old man with a beard or present a blank page. For young children, a blank page is not evidence of abstract theology, but nothing more than an empty sheet of paper. *God's Paintbrush* helps to fill in the blank page with colorful images which move beyond the kindly bearded gentleman.

The answers to the questions at the end of each page are inside each reader. The conversation they spark is more important than any one response. In the end, the most important lesson of the book is the realization that God's colors are in us, and we can paint with God's paintbrush.

2

The Theological Foundations of *God's Paintbrush*

Rabbi Jeffrey L. Schein

God's Paintbrush is based on a positive evaluation of a child's image-making capacity. Too often theologians have responded to a child's developmental need for concrete images of God by forbidding those images as anthropomorphic misrepresentations of an imageless God. Religion then becomes a taboo area where we restrain what is otherwise a great source of energy and creativity for children. Rabbi Sasso takes a different tack. I believe she helps us embark on a journey where we come to appreciate the infinite nature of God by extending, not squashing, our image-making capacity.

In order to expand the child's repertoire of images of Godliness, Rabbi Sasso relies on three theological building blocks of Jewish tradition:

1. People are made in God's image—*Betzelem Elohim.* We can begin to think that there is a correspondence between our best actions and God's nature because we believe that there is something of the divine image in each of us. This theological construct invites constant dialogue about the nature of the divine-human resemblance, suggesting from the beginning that the resemblance is non-physical and must reside in our deepest emotional and spiritual human qualities.

2. We are God's partners in the ongoing creation of the world—*Shitufey adonay bema'asey bereshit.* We can ask children, as Rabbi Sasso does in the story, how our actions affect God, and how God affects us, precisely because we are viewed as partners in life.

3. Jewish tradition recognizes that the Torah speaks in the "language of human beings"—*Bilshon b'nai adam.* It is the only language we own and thus becomes a sanctioned tool for exploring our relationship with God. Perhaps the worst theological trick that has ever been played on us is to cause us to think that there is a perfect, abstract language of theological discourse. When this happens, we give up on the poetic and imaginative language so present and accessible for children.

The interaction of these three Jewish concepts about God's nature and relationship to human beings is constant and subtle in the book. By rooting *God's Paintbrush* in such rich theological soil, Rabbi Sasso unleashes the potential for the educator and child to create new pages of the book as they journey through God's world.

Using *God's Paintbrush* Creatively and Flexibly

Rabbi Jeffrey L. Schein

Children between the ages of five and nine are the best readership for *God's Paintbrush*. At home in a parent's lap or tucked into bed, the parent and child will respond to one another organically. No lessons need be planned.

But it is our experience that in a religious or day school setting, *God's Paintbrush* needs special handling. It is a book that is not intended to be assimilated in one reading, particularly if children are passive listeners. Thus, teachers should be aware of different ways in which sections of the book can be presented and techniques of storytelling altered. *God's Paintbrush* is also a volume that points beyond itself. Teachers should be aware of the possibility of utilizing the volume for units of study or as an organizing center for year-long discussion about God and the world.

Below are a set of suggestions in regard to these challenges:

1. Allow for visual and verbal interpretation. After having read several pages to the students, ask them to use their own words to describe the element of God in the picture. Also let them explore the visual images in the text. Exactly where is God in this picture: Inside the person? In the beauty?

2. Children have their own "paintbrushes." Read the book in segments and invite children to create their own picture after hearing several examples.

3. Vary the pace of the book. Some pictures have questions after the text and others do not. If you want to move quickly through the book, skip the questions. If you want to spend more time on the presence of God in this action or scene, ask the question in a way that is not rhetorical. Pause and explore with the children.

4. These texts can be revisited as the cycle of the holiday year unfolds. Pictures of celebration and silliness can be returned to at Purim; forgiveness at Easter or Rosh Hashanah and Yom Kippur; free-to-be-myself at Pesah.

5. Invite children to extend the text via a mural. Periodically during the year they can draw new pictures representing their new discoveries of God.

Teaching Suggestions for Jewish Educators

Alice Weinstein

The use of metaphor is how Rabbi Sandy Eisenberg Sasso assists children to think and converse about God in *God's Paintbrush*. Metaphor is "a common, everyday technique for talking about objects or events in terms appropriate to other objects or events. It is the presentation of...facts of one sort as if they belong to another [category]."[1] Metaphor is especially useful in talking about God because it helps provide teacher and students with accessible language for discussing a difficult and abstract topic. A conversation about God is virtually impossible using only logic and literal language. "With metaphor a person can bring new insights to a situation. An apt metaphor provides a vision and meaning that otherwise would elude us."[2] Using analogy or metaphor puts the discussion within a "frame of reference [which] is a comparison model that encourages [the students] to draw parallels between familiar experience and the material to be learned."[3]

Metaphor can be a way of "making the strange familiar and is designed to make new, unfamiliar ideas more meaningful." Using metaphor in this way, *God's Paintbrush* asks children to look at the world and the people around them and to see God in their everyday experiences and relationships. As a result:

1. *God's Paintbrush* becomes a tool that enables a teacher to create a comfortable environment in which children can feel encouraged to connect their lives with what is sacred.

2. The playfulness of the metaphor-making process helps students and educators together to discover new sacred communications.

The book is rich in the potential for individual lessons that can span an entire semester, or even a year, of religious school. Though some of the concepts are presented on a seemingly elementary level, the topics are germane through the entire breadth of grades.

Suggestions for the Jewish Classroom

INTRODUCTION: When introducing the unit using *God's Paintbrush* as a vehicle for starting "God talk" in the classroom, begin with a discussion of how the students would describe God. Explain that one of the ways the author of the book has cho-

1   Hyman, Ronald T., *Ways of Teaching,* Second Edition (Philadelphia: J.B. Lippincott Company, 1974).
2   *Ibid*, p. 32.
3   Hayes, David A., *A Sourcebook of Interactive Methods for Teaching with Texts* (Boston: Allyn & Bacon, 1992), 72.

sen is to compare God to a painter or artist.

Ask: To what other occupation might you compare God? (Examples: builder, farmer, scientist, sculptor, road builder, author, cook, etc.)

Have the students talk about why they chose a particular occupation. How is God like a builder? An author? A cook?

EXAMPLE: Speak about God as if God were a composer and orchestra conductor. (Make a sign for each student with words or pictures of the things God created during the Creation narrative and have a baton available. Distribute the signs and designate one student as the conductor. Allow him/her to practice waving his/her arms like an orchestra conductor.)

Have this student "conduct" the parts of Creation by having the students stand up with their signs as he/she points to them. At the end, all will be standing and Creation will be complete.

CONCLUSION: Now that we have acted out one way that we may talk about God, we may feel it is easier to talk about God as if God is a painter with a giant paintbrush.

God as an Artist, page 4

At the beginning of the book, after discussing the sunbeam and the rainbow, supply the students with watercolors. On a large sheet of white mural paper, allow them to paint their world. Encourage large strokes, and suggest that they blend the colors together to make new colors. Explain that the mural does not have to show definite objects, but can be abstract, if they choose.

Night Light, page 5

Discuss the children's feelings at night. Allow them to role play in order to express themselves. Assure them that no one will laugh if they talk about things that make them afraid in the dark and allow their peers to suggest comforting ways they may want to handle these fears.

Have the students close their eyes and tell you what they feel in the dark "behind their eyelids." Are they seeing the same pictures they see at night after the lights are out?

This provides a further opportunity to discuss Creation with them. The book asks if God made the stars and moon as the night light for the other things in nature. Share the *midrash* (rabbinic commentary on the Bible) of R. Simeon ben Pazzi regarding the moon, or the story of R. Aha about the stars: [4]

The Moon:

> R. Simeon ben Pazzi pointed out a [seeming] contradiction between two parts of the same verse. The verse begins by saying, "And God made the two great lights" (Gen. 1:16), and then goes on to speak of "a greater light...and a lesser light". [However, this is what happened]: The moon dared to say to the Holy One, "Master of the universe, is it possible for two kings to wear the same size crown?" The Holy One answered, "Go, then, and make yourself smaller." But the moon protested, "Master of the universe, must I make myself smaller merely because I suggested to You something that is sensible?" The Holy One conceded, "Very well. Go and rule by day[5] as well as by night."[6]

The Stars:

> "And the stars" (Gen. 1:16). R. Aha said: [The association of the stars with the moon] will be understood by the parable of a king who had two administrators, one ruling in the city and the other ruling the [rest of the] province. The king said: Since one was willing to be diminished to rule only the city, I decree that whenever he goes forth, the city council and the populace shall go forth with him, and whenever he returns, the city council and the populace shall return with him. So, too, did the Holy One: Since the moon was willing to be diminished and to rule by night, I, [said God], decree that when she comes forth, the stars shall go forth with her, and when she returns, the stars shall return with her.[7]

God's Sadness and Joy, pages 6 & 7

> Ask the students if they ever feel as if their day is "dark or cloudy." Explain that it is normal and all right if every day is not perfect. We know that the weather changes from rainy and cloudy one day to bright and sunny the next. In the same way, things that happen to us one day may be sad, or frightening, but there are also good days, and we feel "sunny" again.

> Open a discussion of things the students know that happen in the

4 Bialik, Hayim Nachman and Yehoshua Hana Ravnitsky, eds., *The Book of Legends — Sefer Ha'aggadah* (New York: Schocken Books, 1992).
5 The moon is at times visible during the day.
6 B. Hul 60b
7 Gen. R. 6:9

world today that would make God cry, e.g., homelessness, hunger, sickness, or war. Then discuss the converse — when does God laugh, or even smile? How can they, as children, do things that they think will make God smile or laugh?

In this exercise, the teacher can connect the things that the students suggest to Jewish values — *mitzvot* (commandments), *gemilut hasidim* (deeds of lovingkindness), *tzedakah* (giving), *Bikur Holim* (visiting the sick), *Bal Tashchit* (caring for the environment), and *tefillah* (prayer).

God's Pain, pages 8 & 9

When discussing the word "hurt," differentiate between physical hurting (injury or pain) and hurting inside (feelings, sadness). Explain that the physical hurt can often be taken care of by a doctor with bandages or medicine. The hurt inside is harder to see and to treat. Ask the students when they hurt inside. Do words other people speak hurt them? Do they say or do things that will hurt other people? When you hurt other people are you being a good friend? Are you hurting God?

Explain that sometimes we can make others feel better by writing letters to them, just like the boy in the book. In one exercise, instruct the students to write a letter to God, trying to make God feel better about things that might hurt. The letter also might say how the children can be a better "friend" to God. In another exercise invite students to write to someone they have hurt, to ask for forgiveness.

God's Echo, pages 10 & 11

Explain that God created people to make the world a better place. In that way we are God's echo, because we are doing what God would do to make the world better. The Torah tells us that we were created in God's image. Therefore, what we do is a reflection of God.

Instruct the children to fold a paper in half and make an "echo" picture, one half being the mirror image of the other.

God as Friend, pages 12 & 13

Talk about being God's partner. Ask children to roleplay being a friend to a new person in your class. What would the children do so that their hands would be like God's hands? Have the person playing the stranger express his/her feelings at being new, or a stranger.

In open discussion, ask the students if and when they have ever felt that they did not belong or were alone. At this point, the teacher should bring out the concept that we are never really alone because God is always with us.

God as Parent, pages 14 & 15

On the pages which talk about parents, have the students describe times when they felt very comfortable and loved. When they think of God, do they also feel comfortable and loved?

Assure children that the child that broke the vase was still loved by his/her parents. Even when we make mistakes, our parents still love us. If God made us, then God is like our parent, too.

God's Song, pages 16 –18

Ask students what they hear when they hear the wind. Does it say anything to them? Does it ever sound like music?

Moving like the wind is fun. Have the students stand up and improvise moving like the wind. The wind makes the tree branches and the leaves dance. Make your movements into a wind dance. Ask if any child would like to make up a wind song that they can sing while they move like the wind. Make your song beautiful — a tune for God's wind. (At this point, the teacher may want to start a simple *niggun* — a wordless melody — that the children may move to.)

Next ask the children what words they would put in God's song. Would the words be God talking to them, or would they like to talk to God? Explain that talking to God is called praying: What would they like to say to God? We pray for God to help us and we bless God for all the things God has made and done for us. After the children are seated, ask them what words they use to bless God (*Baruch atah...*) and what are some of the blessings that they know (*Kiddush*, lighting the *Shabbat* candles, *motzi...*). Have students write their own prayer.

God's Touch, page 19

Ask children what they like to touch. What things feel good to touch? God made all things, so when we touch and hug and have good feelings, it is a way that we are touching God.

One way that God wants us to touch other people is by helping them.

The ways that we are supposed to help are called *mitzvot* — God's commandments. The way that we touch other people is a way of helping God. Ask students how people touch God by:

- Visiting the sick (*Bikur Holim*)
- Honoring parents (*Kibud Av V'Imah*)
- Teaching one another (*Limud Torah*)

God's Dance, pages 20 & 21

When we danced before, we danced as the wind. How would you picture God's dance — joyous, happy, solemn, with big steps, little steps, fast or slow? What music would you use to dance God's dance?

Have students create their own dance as they imagine how God wants them to dance.

God and Changes, pages 22 & 23

Have students close their eyes and picture in their minds how they looked when they were babies. Then ask students to picture themselves as they started to walk, to talk, to ride a tricycle, to climb.... What differences do students see in themselves now from when they were toddlers, or even when they were in nursery school? How do they imagine themselves looking when they are grown up?

Supply students with paper and crayons or markers and have them draw themselves at these four stages in their lives (i.e., babies, toddlers, elementary school, high school). Have the students use the pictures to talk about the way they change and grow.

God and Creation, pages 26 & 27

When God created the world, God made each thing in creation unique. There are no two things *exactly* alike. God also made each person different from every other person.

We should be proud of ourselves for the things that we can do. What special ability or talent has God given you that makes you proud?

Supply a large mirror, full length if possible. Have each student look into the mirror and tell one special thing that they like best about themselves. Those things can be how a part of us looks, what we do well, what we like to do.

Rejoicing with God, pages 27 & 29

We all play on a playground sometimes. Playing is fun and makes us happy. If God were to take time to play on a playground, what would it look like? Using paper and crayons/markers, ask students to draw a playground for God. Perhaps the things in it would all be natural, or maybe unusual objects would be used for the playthings instead of what we are used to seeing. The important thing is to be imaginative.

God's Eyes, pages 30 & 31

Do you think that everyone sees things exactly the same way? When two people look at a picture, or out of a window, each of them sees different things first. Do you notice objects first, or do you notice people first? When you look at people, do you try to figure out if they are happy or sad, lonely, mean...? Looking at someone's eyes is sometimes a good way to figure out what they are feeling.

If God were looking at *you* what kind of person would God see? How do you think God sees the world around us? Are God's eyes happy or sad when God sees the world?

God as Creator, page 32

We started the book by painting a mural of the world using the colors that might be in God's paintbrush. Now we know that we can help God by being painters for God. The beauty in the world doesn't have to come just with paints. Good deeds, kindness, friendship, love, music, ... are all part of God's palette of colors. We can make God's world even brighter and more colorful through what we do.

FOR OLDER STUDENTS:

Ask students to compose a list of wishes for the future. What would they like to change or make better in the world if they had the power to do so?

Ask them to begin with the statement, "If I could be God's paintbrush for a day, I would...." Ask students to share their thoughts with the class.

FOR YOUNGER STUDENTS:

Ask students to draw a wish for the future if they could use God's paintbrush. What would they like to change or make better if they had the power to do so?

These creative exercises would make a good bulletin board display for the unit's culmination. The title for the bulletin board might be "If We Had a Chance at *Tikkun Olam* — Repairing the World."

Teaching Suggestions for Christian Educators

Elizabeth McMahon Jeep

We cannot give faith to our children; only God can offer that treasure. But we can reveal our own hearts to the children we love. We can tell them what we see when we look at the world with the eyes of faith. We can invite them to share in activities that are the response of faithful people: Prayer, care and celebration.

Each page of the book *God's Paintbrush* provides rich material for conversations and celebrations that give children access to our religious understandings and commitments. One way we do this is through the simple and time-honored method of reading a book together, and talking over with our children the ideas and experiences that the book brings to mind. It can be used in either a home or congregational setting.

To engage children in conversation we ordinarily need only to ask questions and to be good listeners — and avoid the temptation to become preachy or moralistic. The pictures and text can help us combat that tendency. With a brief question or comment about the realities portrayed in the painting, we initiate the conversation. "What do you see in the picture? Have you done something like that? Have you ever felt that way? What do the words ask us?" Allow time for their stories and questions, and linger over the "I wonder how..." and "I wonder why..." sentences. Guided by the children's responses, we move from a concrete experience to a discussion of the way it reveals or relates us to God.

The conversation itself will usually suggest a deepening activity, such as drawing a picture or singing a psalm. This response takes the conversation beyond mere words. It provides an opportunity to affirm in a personal way, the experience of the Transcendent that is being explored. This "experiential" element is seldom neglected in the Sunday school setting, but it should be an important part of informal family gatherings as well.

CONVERSATION AND CELEBRATION

> Bible references are from the *New Revised Standard Version*, Oxford University Press, 1989; psalm references may differ in other translations.

Page 3

God is playful, an awesome but desirable presence. Creation is a continuous, changing process. Creatures are given life and movement of their own. They change, disappear. They delight God. Humans are also creative (fence, farm, auto). Do we delight in/care for the things we create?

Watch the clouds today. Learn Psalm 36:5 — "Your steadfast love, O Lord, extends to the heavens, your faithfulness to the clouds."

Pages 4 & 5

Contrasts in nature reflect contrasting emotions. All can lead us to God the Creator. Why do we call Christ the "Light of the World"? How do the candles of Christmas and Easter tell this "good news"?

Read the first story of creation, especially days 1 and 4 (Genesis 1:1-2:3). Make rainbows with paint or prisms. Watch the night sky. Talk about night lights. Learn Psalm 18:28 — "It is you who light my lamp; the Lord, my God, lights up my darkness."

Pages 6 & 7

More contrasts and more emotions to be explored. Read about the variety and balance of life (Ecclesiastes 3:1-4). Ocean water is powerful; it carries many forms of life. How is it like the water of baptism?

Tell some jokes, tickle the end of your nose with some shaving cream. Visit the baptismal font. Learn Romans 12:15 — "Rejoice with those who rejoice, weep with those who weep."

Pages 8 & 9

Does God experience emotions? Some philosophers think of God as unchangeable serenity. But mystics use rich imagery to describe a God whose love is a strongly felt emotion.

Read about the time when Jesus wept (shorten the story: John 11:1- 7, 20-44). Write to a friend or relative. Learn Matthew 5:4 — "Blessed are those who mourn, for they will be comforted."

Pages 10 & 11

When do our words carry joy and blessing? When do they hurt others? God speaks through nature, the Bible, the church, parents, siblings, and friends.

Read about the boy who heard God's call (I Samuel 3:1-10). Sing an echo song (a round). Whisper good words in someone's ear. Learn the good news of our faith: Matthew 16:15-17—"Jesus said to them, 'But who do you say that I am?' Simon Peter answered, 'You are the Messiah, the Son of the living God.' And Jesus answered him, 'Blessed are you, Simon son of Jonah! For flesh and blood has not revealed this to you, but My Father in heaven.'"

Pages 12 & 13

How do we "give a hand" with the laundry? When someone falls? When we see a play? Do we sometimes hurt others with our hands? How do our hands care for pets? What does it mean that we are made "in God's image"?

Read about the good shepherd (Matthew 18:12-14). We belong to God; who else belongs to God's family? Learn Psalm 31:5 — "Into your hand I commit my spirit; you have redeemed me, O Lord, faithful God."

Pages 14 & 15

It can be difficult, even for children, to live with a God who is both near and far away, who speaks and yet is silent. We strive for faith that is steady and confident. It helps us in bad times, but does not prevent bad times and loneliness from happening. Loving adults are both an image and a channel of Divine Love.

On one piece of paper, trace the hands of all those who help you. Smile at someone who seems lonely. Read about the promise of Jesus (John 16:16-22). Learn Isaiah 41:10 — "Do not fear, for I am with you. Do not be afraid, for I am your God; I will strengthen you, I will help you, I will uphold you with My victorious right hand."

Pages 16 & 17

God's breath shared with us is life, is grace. God's spirit is breathed on us, filling us with strength and making us one.

Read about the coming of God's Spirit in fire and wind (shorten the story:

Acts 2:1-6, 12-17, 21). Have a picnic, sing songs, dance. Make a wind chime, fly a kite. Learn Job 33:4 — "The spirit of God has made me, and the breath of the Almighty gives me life."

Pages 18 & 19

Each sense is a doorway to the sacred: We hear God's song, we feel God's touch. What sounds make us happy, sad, excited? What would the world be like without things that are scratchy, smooth, cold, prickly, sticky? How does God delight us through the gifts of taste, sight, smell, memory, imagination?

Tape the sounds of your world. Play some music. Learn a new hymn. Learn the words of Isaiah 66:12-13 — "Thus says the Lord: As a mother comforts her child, so I will comfort you."

Pages 20 & 21

The stars carried messages to Abraham (Genesis 22:15-17) and to the Wise Men (Matthew 2:1-11). What do they tell you?

Read Psalm 148; make up more verses. Name some constellations; share star legends. Do a "dance of Abraham and the Wise Men." Learn Psalm 148:1, 3—"Praise the Lord from the heavens; praise him in the heights! Praise him, sun and moon; praise him, all you shining stars!"

Pages 22 & 23

All growth involves loss; all life involves death; all resurrection involves suffering. Each is part of the dance. What examples of these elements have the children experienced?

Measure your height. Give away something you have outgrown. Dream about what you will do when you grow up. Plant some seeds and watch them grow. Learn John 12:24 — "Unless a grain of wheat falls into the earth and dies, it remains just a single grain; but if it dies, it bears much fruit."

Pages 24 & 25

God has many helpers: Parents, grandparents, aunts, uncles, teachers,

bus drivers, librarians. How do we help God help others? How do members of the church take up the mission of Jesus?

Discuss the prayer that calls God "our Father." Discuss other biblical images of God's presence, such as a mother bird (Psalm 17:8) or a solid rock (Psalm 18:2). Learn Psalm 16:8 — "I keep the Lord always before me; because he is at my right hand, I shall not be moved."

Pages 26 & 27

We use our many gifts at school, at home, and with our friends. What do you like to do? What do you do well? Gifts are meant to be shared, not compared.

Tell someone the good things you see in them. Read a story about talents and opportunities (Matthew 25:14-27). Learn Colossians 3:17 — "Whatever you do, in word or deed, do everything in the name of the Lord Jesus, giving thanks to God the Father through Him."

Pages 28 & 29

We are not as careful about the earth as we should be. How do we use and enjoy things without destroying them?

Take a nature walk; notice as many colors as you can. Name five beautiful things about your neighborhood. Think of 20 ways to play with a jar lid. Learn Isaiah 55:12 — "The mountains and the hills before you shall burst into song, and all the trees of the field shall clap their hands."

Pages 30 & 31

Children reflect the competitiveness and prejudices of their elders. Are there lonely people in the family, school or neighborhood — people who never get a smile or a "thank you"? What can we do to make them feel better?

Help someone today. Give lots of "thank you's" today. Learn John 13:34-35 — "Just as I have loved you, you also should love one another. By this everyone will know that you are My disciples, if you have love for one another."

Page 32:

What color is God's caring? God's forgiving? God's imagination? God's happiness? God's interest in what we have to say? God's love?

Think beautiful thoughts. Paint a beautiful picture; give it to someone special. Wear your favorite colors. Eat something orange and something green. Learn I John 4:16 — "God is love, and those who abide in love abide in God, and God abides in them."

God's Paintbrush and *Tikkun Olam* (Repairing the World):
A Family Program

Rabbi Jeffrey L. Schein & Renée Frank Holtz

God's Paintbrush can be used in the context of family education. Parents as well as children need permission to explore their relationship to God. Seeing God through their child's wondering eyes can help parents revisit the role of God in their own lives. Further, such a program provides an opportunity for families to engage in God talk in ways which, it is hoped, will lead to further dialogue in their home.

This program, with its emphasis on *Tikkun Olam* (repairing the world), was designed originally for second graders and their parents. It could easily be adapted to grades K - 4.

ACTIVITIES

1. Can you draw God? It's difficult!

   Can you instead draw one thing that you think God does here on earth? Parents and children should share with one another the pictures they have drawn. Each family might then share its pictures with one other family.

2. In the book *God's Paintbrush*, we are told that our hands can help God's hands [page 10]. The child relates that "my Mom and I went shopping in the city.... How can your hands help God's hands?"

   In Judaism we call helping God *Tikkun Olam*, repairing the world. How many ways can you think of to help God fix the world? Parents and students should be given a photocopied map of the world. On the map families can draw pictures of some of the "cracks" (bad things) in the world. Each family is then given a Band Aid with a small piece of paper attached to it. On the Band Aid the family writes one thing they can do as a family that might lead to *Tikkun Olam*.

3. On pages 16 & 17, *God's Paintbrush* says:

> "When the wind blows warm, making grass, trees and flowers dance, it makes my hair brush against my face. I think the wind is God's breath moving through the world, making it come alive.
>
> I think that God's breath moves through me, too. That makes me special, having a little bit of God inside me. That makes everyone special, having God's breath inside them. We can make words and music with God's breath."

Have everyone be silent, then take a deep breath in and let it out. Can you hear what you are doing? What causes us to do this? Is there a time when your family just enjoys quietly being with one another without talking?

Now cup your hands over your nose and mouth. Do you feel the warmth of your breath? How is God's presence gentle and warm, like breath?

4. Everyone has something that makes them special, makes them closer to God. The child in the story we've been reading says on pages 26 and 27, "My friend is great at math. She always gets 100.... What is your gift? How do you share your gift?"

Everyone take a minute and think about your gift. Show the rest of the group your gift without using words (act it out and have the others guess the gift). Talk about a gift your family offers other people (warmth, friendship, *Shabbat* dinners, holidays, including friends in family outings, etc.).

5. In the beginning we drew a picture of one thing that God does here on earth. Now, let's draw a mural of what the world would be like if it was completely repaired, and the work of *Tikkun Olam* was finished. Title the mural "*Yamot Hamashiah*," messianic times. On the mural of messianic times, each family can write a concluding note of what they most enjoyed about the program.

This program was originally developed in a different format by Renée Frank Holtz with guidance by Dr. Sherry Blumberg. The original program utilized many multi-sensory activities like those described in Alice Weinstein's and Elizabeth Jeep's articles.

Suggestions for Further Reading

Rabbi Jeffrey L. Schein & Rabbi Sandy Eisenberg Sasso

There are a number of texts available for educators and parents who would like to learn more about children's spirituality and their relationship to God. We recommend the following books.

Coles, Robert. *The Spiritual Life of Children*. Boston: Houghton Mifflin Company, 1990.

> Seeks to open a window to a child's spiritual life. Robert Coles works very hard to allow children to speak in their own voices. He interviews hundreds of children about their understanding of God's voice, God's commands and demands, and most of all the special relationship each has to God.

Fitzpatrick, Jeanne Grasso. *Something More: Nurturing Your Child's Spiritual Growth*. New York: Viking Penguin, 1991.

> Full of very concrete ideas for nurturing spirituality with children. It has a wonderful way of pointing out the spiritually educable moments we normally miss as parents and teachers.

Kushner, Harold. *When Children Ask About God*. New York: Reconstructionist Press, 1971.

> This book has something of the character of a Maimonadean Guide to the Perplexed for teacher or parent. The consistent theme of the book is to "know what a child is really asking" when you feel challenged or stumped by his/her questions about God.

Other Books to Promote Teachers' Understanding

Fowler, James W. *Stages of Faith: The Psychology of Human Development and the Quest for Meaning.* San Francisco: Harper & Row, 1991.

Gellman, Rabbi Marc, and Monsignor Thomas Hartman. *Where Does God Live? Questions and Answers for Parents and Children.* New York: Triumph Books, 1991.

Heller, David. *The Children's God.* Chicago: The University Press, 1986.

_____. *Talking to Your Child about God: A Book for Families of All Faiths.* New York: Bantam Books, 1988.

Hull, John M. *God-Talk with Young Children.* Philadelphia: Trinity Press, 1991.

Olitzky, Kerry M., Steven M. Rosman and David P. Kasakove. *When Your Jewish Child Asks Why: Answers for Tough Questions.* Hoboken, N.J.: KTAV, 1993.

Wolpe, David J. *Teaching Your Children about God: A Modern Jewish Approach.* New York: Henry Holt and Company, 1993.

Books for Sharing with Children

For a complete listing of books by Sandy Eisenberg Sasso (all useful for classroom discussion), see pages 24–26.

Boroson, Martin. *Becoming Me: A Story of Creation.* Woodstock, Vt.: SkyLight Paths Publishing, 1999.

The 11th Commandment: Wisdom from Our Children. Woodstock, Vt.: Jewish Lights Publishing, 1996.

Gold, August, and Matthew J. Perlman. *Where Does God Live?* Woodstock, Vt.: SkyLight Paths Publishing, 2001.

Kushner, Lawrence and Karen. *Because Nothing Looks Like God.* Woodstock, Vt.: Jewish Lights Publishing, 2000.

Landy, Robert J. *God Lives in Glass: Reflections of God through the Eyes of Children.* Woodstock, Vt.: SkyLight Paths Publishing, 2001.

Sasso, Sandy Eisenberg. *God's Paintbrush Celebration Kit.* Woodstock, Vt.: Jewish Lights Publishing, 1999.

Swartz, Nancy Sohn. *In Our Image: God's First Creatures.* Woodstock, Vt.: Jewish Lights Publishing, 1998.

Wood, Douglas. *Old Turtle.* Duluth, Minn.: Pfeifer-Hamilton, 1991.

About the Contributors

Rabbi Jeffrey L. Schein is a professor of Jewish education at the Cleveland College of Jewish Studies and the national education director of the Jewish Reconstructionist Federation. His publications include four books and several dozen articles regarding Jewish education.

Rabbi Joseph M. Blair graduated with ordination from the Reconstructionist Rabbinical College. He has served as co-editor for *Windows on the Jewish Soul* and *Connecting Prayer and Spirituality* (both Jewish Reconstructionist Federation), as assistant editor for *Kol Haneshamah: Siddur Limot Hol/Daily* (JRF), and as the editor of the JRF Education Newsletter. He has taught the second through seventh grades over the past ten years, as well as adults. He is currently serving as rabbi at Congregation Ner Tamid in Voorhees, New Jersey. He holds master's degrees in Hebrew letters and computer science, and a Juris Doctorate degree.

Renée Frank Holtz is the director of education at Congregation Kol Ami (formerly the Jewish Community Center) in White Plains, New York, where she supervises the religious school and youth departments. She has an M.S.Ed. in special education from Johns Hopkins University and an M.A. from Baltimore Hebrew University. Having directed several schools, she focuses much of her time on family education at all levels and enjoys teaching students and parents together.

Elizabeth McMahon Jeep is a writer, lecturer, and consultant in the field of religious education and children's worship. She has an M.A. from the Catholic University of America, and is completing doctoral work at The Chicago Theological Seminary. She and her husband make their home in River Forest, Illinois.

Rabbi Sandy Eisenberg Sasso is author of the acclaimed *God's Paintbrush* and other inspiring books for children of all faiths, all backgrounds. Her award-winning books include: *Cain & Abel: Finding the Fruits of Peace; For Heaven's Sake; God Said Amen; God in Between; In God's Name; But God Remembered: Stories of Women from Creation to the Promised Land;* and *A Prayer for the Earth: The Story of Naamah, Noah's Wife* (all Jewish Lights). She is a parent, spiritual leader, and storyteller, and is active in the interfaith community. The second woman to be ordained as a rabbi (1974) and the first rabbi to become a mother, she and her husband, Dennis, were the first rabbinical couple to jointly lead a congregation—Beth-El Zedeck in Indianapolis.

Alice Weinstein is a teacher and program coordinator. She is currently completing her B.J.S. and Executive Educator Certificate from the Cleveland College of Jewish Studies, and is chair of the CAJE (Coalition for the Advancement of Jewish Education) Tzedakah Network, and co-chair of the CAJE Music Network.

About Jewish Lights Publishing

People of all faiths and backgrounds yearn for books that attract, engage, educate, and spiritually inspire.

Our principal goal is to stimulate thought and help all people learn about who the Jewish People are, where they come from, and what the future can be made to hold. While people of our diverse Jewish heritage are the primary audience, our books speak to people in the Christian world as well and will broaden their understanding of Judaism and the roots of their own faith.

We bring to you authors who are at the forefront of spiritual thought and experience. While each has something different to say, they all say it in a voice that you can hear.

Our books are designed to welcome you and then to engage, stimulate, and inspire. We judge our success not only by whether or not our books are beautiful and commercially successful, but by whether or not they make a difference in your life.

Life Cycle & Holidays

How to Be a Perfect Stranger, 2nd Ed. In 2 Volumes
A Guide to Etiquette in Other People's Religious Ceremonies
Ed. by *Stuart M. Matlins* & *Arthur J. Magida*   AWARD WINNER!

What will happen? What do I do? What do I wear? What do I say? What are their basic beliefs? Should I bring a gift? Explains the rituals and celebrations of North America's major religions/denominations, helping an interested guest to feel comfortable. *Not* presented from the perspective of any particular faith.
SKYLIGHT PATHS Books
Vol. 1: *North America's Largest Faiths,* 6 x 9, 432 pp, Quality PB, ISBN 1-893361-01-2
Vol. 2: *Other Faiths in North America,* 6 x 9, 416 pp, Quality PB, ISBN 1-893361-02-0

Celebrating Your New Jewish Daughter
Creating Jewish Ways to Welcome Baby Girls into the Covenant— New and Traditional Ceremonies

by *Debra Nussbaum Cohen;* Foreword by *Rabbi Sandy Eisenberg Sasso*

Features everything families need to plan a celebration that reflects Jewish tradition, including a how-to guide to new and traditional ceremonies, and practical guidelines for planning the joyous event. 6 x 9, 272 pp, Quality PB, ISBN 1-58023-090-3

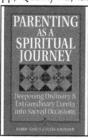

The New Jewish Baby Book   AWARD WINNER!
Names, Ceremonies & Customs—A Guide for Today's Families
by Anita Diamant 6 x 9, 336 pp, Quality PB, ISBN 1-879045-28-1
Parenting As a Spiritual Journey
Deepening Ordinary & Extraordinary Events into Sacred Occasions
by Rabbi Nancy Fuchs-Kreimer 6 x 9, 224 pp, Quality PB, ISBN 1-58023-016-4
Putting God on the Guest List, 2nd Ed.   AWARD WINNER!
How to Reclaim the Spiritual Meaning of Your Child's Bar or Bat Mitzvah
by Rabbi Jeffrey K. Salkin 6 x 9, 224 pp, Quality PB, ISBN 1-879045-59-1
For Kids—Putting God on Your Guest List
How to Claim the Spiritual Meaning of Your Bar or Bat Mitzvah
by Rabbi Jeffrey K. Salkin 6 x 9, 144 pp, Quality PB, ISBN 1-58023-015-6
Bar/Bat Mitzvah Basics, 2nd Ed.: *A Practical Family Guide to Coming of Age Together*
Ed. by Cantor Helen Leneman 6 x 9, 240 pp, Quality PB, ISBN 1-58023-151-9
Hanukkah, 2nd Ed.: The Family Guide to Spiritual Celebration: The Art of Jewish Living
by Dr. Ron Wolfson 7 x 9, 240 pp, Quality PB, Illus., ISBN 1-58023-122-5
The Shabbat Seder: The Art of Jewish Living
by Dr. Ron Wolfson 7 x 9, 272 pp, Quality PB, Illus., ISBN 1-879045-90-7
The Passover Seder: The Art of Jewish Living
by Dr. Ron Wolfson 7 x 9, 352 pp, Quality PB, Illus., ISBN 1-879045-93-1

Children's Spirituality

Because Nothing Looks Like God

by *Lawrence and Karen Kushner*
Full-color illus. by *Dawn W. Majewski*

For ages 4 & up

MULTICULTURAL, NONDENOMINATIONAL, NONSECTARIAN

What is God like? The first collaborative work by husband-and-wife team Lawrence and Karen Kushner introduces children to the possibilities of spiritual life. Real-life examples of happiness and sadness—from goodnight stories, to the hope and fear felt the first time at bat, to the closing moments of life—invite us to explore, together with our children, the questions we all have about God, no matter what our age.

11 x 8½, 32 pp, HC, Full-color illus., ISBN 1-58023-092-X

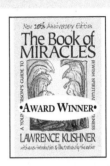

Where Is God?
What Does God Look Like?
How Does God Make Things Happen? (Board Books)

For ages 0–4

by *Lawrence and Karen Kushner;* Full-color illus. by *Dawn W. Majewski*

Gently invites children to become aware of God's presence all around them. Three board books abridged from *Because Nothing Looks Like God* by Lawrence and Karen Kushner.
Each 5 x 5, 24 pp, Board, Full-color illus. SKYLIGHT PATHS Books

Sharing Blessings

Children's Stories for Exploring the Spirit of the Jewish Holidays

For ages 6 & up

by *Rahel Musleah* and *Rabbi Michael Klayman*
Full-color illus. by *Mary O'Keefe Young*

What is the spiritual message of each of the Jewish holidays? How do we teach it to our children? Many books tell children about the historical significance and customs of the holidays. Through stories about one family's preparation, *Sharing Blessings* explores ways to get into the *spirit* of 13 different holidays.
8½ x 11, 64 pp, HC, Full-color illus., ISBN 1-879045-71-0

The Book of Miracles

A Young Person's Guide to Jewish Spiritual Awareness

For ages 9 & up

by *Lawrence Kushner*

Introduces kids to a way of everyday spiritual thinking to last a lifetime. Kushner, whose award-winning books have brought spirituality to life for countless adults, now shows young people how to use Judaism as a foundation on which to build their lives.
6 x 9, 96 pp, HC, 2-color illus., ISBN 1-879045-78-8

Children's Spirituality

In Our Image
God's First Creatures
by *Nancy Sohn Swartz*

Full-color illus. by *Melanie Hall*

For ages 4 & up

A playful new twist on the Creation story—from the perspective of the animals. Celebrates the interconnectedness of nature and the harmony of all living things. "The vibrantly colored illustrations nearly leap off the page in this delightful interpretation." —*School Library Journal*

9 x 12, 32 pp, HC, Full-color illus., ISBN 1-879045-99-0

God's Paintbrush

For ages 4 & up

by *Sandy Eisenberg Sasso;* Full-color illus. by *Annette Compton*

Invites children of all faiths and backgrounds to encounter God openly in their own lives. Wonderfully interactive; provides questions adult and child can explore together at the end of each episode.

11 x 8½, 32 pp, HC, Full-color illus., ISBN 1-879045-22-2
Also available: **A Teacher's Guide: A Guide for Jewish & Christian Educators and Parents**
8½ x 11, 32 pp, PB, ISBN 1-879045-57-5

God's Paintbrush Celebration Kit 9½ x 12, HC, Includes 5 sessions/40 full-color Activity Sheets and Teacher Folder with complete instructions, ISBN 1-58023-050-4

In God's Name

For ages 4 & up

by *Sandy Eisenberg Sasso;* Full-color illus. by *Phoebe Stone*

Like an ancient myth in its poetic text and vibrant illustrations, this award-winning modern fable about the search for God's name celebrates the diversity and, at the same time, the unity of all the people of the world.

9 x 12, 32 pp, HC, Full-color illus., ISBN 1-879045-26-5

What Is God's Name? (A Board Book)

For ages 0–4

An abridged board book version of the award-winning *In God's Name.*
5 x 5, 24 pp, Board, Full-color illus., ISBN 1-893361-10-1 A SKYLIGHT PATHS Book

The 11th Commandment: Wisdom from Our Children

For all ages

by *The Children of America*

"If there were an Eleventh Commandment, what would it be?" Children of many religious denominations across America answer this question—in their own drawings and words. "A rare book of spiritual celebration for all people, of all ages, for all time."—*Bookviews*
8 x 10, 48 pp, HC, Full-color illus., ISBN 1-879045-46-X

Children's Spirituality

God Said Amen

For ages 4 & up

by *Sandy Eisenberg Sasso*
Full-color illus. by *Avi Katz*

A warm and inspiring tale of two kingdoms: one overflowing with water but without oil to light its lamps; the other blessed with oil but no water to grow its gardens. The kingdoms' rulers ask God for help but are too stubborn to ask each other. It takes a minstrel, a pair of royal riding-birds and their young keepers, and a simple act of kindness to show that they need only reach out to each other to find God's answer to their prayers.

9 x 12, 32 pp, HC, Full-color illus., ISBN 1-58023-080-6

For Heaven's Sake

For ages 4 & up

by *Sandy Eisenberg Sasso;* Full-color illus. by *Kathryn Kunz Finney*

Everyone talked about heaven: "Thank heavens." "Heaven forbid." "For heaven's sake, Isaiah." But no one would say what heaven was or how to find it. So Isaiah decides to find out, by seeking answers from many different people.
9 x 12, 32 pp, HC, Full-color illus., ISBN 1-58023-054-7

But God Remembered

For ages 8 & up

Stories of Women from Creation to the Promised Land

by *Sandy Eisenberg Sasso;* Full-color illus. by *Bethanne Andersen*

A fascinating collection of four different stories of women only briefly mentioned in biblical tradition and religious texts. Vibrantly brings to life courageous and strong women from ancient tradition; all teach important values through their actions and faith.
9 x 12, 32 pp, HC, Full-color illus., ISBN 1-879045-43-5

God in Between

For ages 4 & up

by *Sandy Eisenberg Sasso;* Full-color illus. by *Sally Sweetland*

If you wanted to find God, where would you look? A magical, mythical tale that teaches that God can be found where we are: within all of us and the relationships between us.
9 x 12, 32 pp, HC, Full-color illus., ISBN 1-879045-86-9

A Prayer for the Earth: The Story of Naamah, Noah's Wife

For ages 4 & up

by *Sandy Eisenberg Sasso;* Full-color illus. by *Bethanne Andersen*

This new story, based on an ancient text, opens readers' religious imaginations to new ideas about the well-known story of the Flood. When God tells Noah to bring the animals of the world onto the ark, God also calls on Naamah, Noah's wife, to save each plant on Earth.
9 x 12, 32 pp, HC, Full-color illus., ISBN 1-879045-60-5

Spirituality

Does the Soul Survive?
A Jewish Journey to Belief in Afterlife, Past Lives & Living with Purpose

by *Rabbi Elie Kaplan Spitz;* Foreword by *Brian L. Weiss, M.D.*

Spitz relates his own experiences and those shared with him by people he has worked with as a rabbi, and shows us that belief in afterlife and past lives, so often approached with reluctance, is in fact true to Jewish tradition. 6 x 9, 288 pp, HC, ISBN 1-58023-094-6

The Women's Torah Commentary: *New Insights from Women Rabbis on the 54 Weekly Torah Portions* Ed. by *Rabbi Elyse Goldstein*

For the first time, women rabbis provide a commentary on the entire Torah. In a week-by-week format; a perfect gift for others, or for yourself.
6 x 9, 496 pp, HC, ISBN 1-58023-076-8

The Gift of Kabbalah
Discovering the Secrets of Heaven, Renewing Your Life on Earth

by *Tamar Frankiel, Ph.D.*

Makes accessible the mysteries of Kabbalah. Traces Kabbalah's evolution in Judaism and shows us its most important gift: a way of revealing the connection between our "everyday" life and the spiritual oneness of the universe. 6 x 9, 256 pp, HC, ISBN 1-58023-108-X

Bringing the Psalms to Life: *How to Understand and Use the Book of Psalms*
by Rabbi Daniel F. Polish 6 x 9, 208 pp, Quality PB, ISBN 1-58023-157-8;
HC, ISBN 1-58023-077-6

The Empty Chair: *Finding Hope and Joy—*
Timeless Wisdom from a Hasidic Master, Rebbe Nachman of Breslov AWARD WINNER!
4 x 6, 128 pp, Deluxe PB, 2-color text, ISBN 1-879045-67-2

The Gentle Weapon: *Prayers for Everyday and Not-So-Everyday Moments*
Adapted from the Wisdom of Rebbe Nachman of Breslov
4 x 6, 144 pp, Deluxe PB, 2-color text, ISBN 1-58023-022-9

Ancient Secrets: *Using the Stories of the Bible to Improve Our Everyday Lives*
by Rabbi Levi Meier, Ph.D. 5½ x 8½, 288 pp, Quality PB, ISBN 1-58023-064-4

Printed in the USA
CPSIA information can be obtained
at www.ICGtesting.com
JSHW050239120923
48275JS00005B/68